The Magic School Bus®
in the Bat Cave

Arnold   Ralphie   Keesha   Phoebe   Carlos   Tim   Wanda   Dorothy Ann

Cartwheel
·B·O·O·K·S·®

SCHOLASTIC INC.

New York   Toronto   London   Auckland   Sydney
Mexico City   New Delhi   Hong Kong   Buenos Aires

Dear Parents,

Welcome to the Scholastic Reader series. We have taken over 80 years of experience with teachers, parents, and children and put it into a program that is designed to match your child's interests and skills.

Level 1—Short sentences and stories made up of words kids can sound out using their phonics skills and words that are important to remember.

Level 2—Longer sentences and stories with words kids need to know and new "big" words that they will want to know.

Level 3—From sentences to paragraphs to longer stories, these books have large "chunks" of text and are made up of a rich vocabulary.

Level 4—First chapter books with more words and fewer pictures.

It is important that children learn to read well enough to succeed in school and beyond. Here are ideas for reading this book with your child:

- Look at the book together. Encourage your child to read the title and make a prediction about the story.
- Read the book together. Encourage your child to sound out words when appropriate. When your child struggles, you can help by providing the word.
- Encourage your child to retell the story. This is a great way to check for comprehension.

Scholastic Readers are designed to support your child's efforts to learn how to read at every age and every stage. Enjoy helping your child learn to read and love to read.

      —Francie Alexander
        Chief Education Officer
        Scholastic Education

Ms. Frizzle

Liz

Written by Jeanette Lane
Illustrated by Robbin Cuddy

Based on *The Magic School Bus* books
written by Joanna Cole and illustrated by Bruce Degen.

The author would like to thank Barbara French,
Science Officer at Bat Conservation International,
www.batcon.org, for her expert advice in preparing this book.

ISBN-13: 978-0-439-89934-5
ISBN-10: 0-439-89934-6

12 11 10 9 8 7 6 5   8/0 9/0 10/0

Designed by Rick DeMonico.

Printed in the U.S.A.   First printing, October 2006

"Let's go to Tim's house and see,"
Ms. Frizzle says.
"My dad is home today. He can help us
find out about the bats," says Tim.

THE FRIZ HAS GONE BATTY!

THAT HAPPENED A LONG TIME AGO.

We all get back on the bus.
The bus starts to change.
Now it is the little-brown-bat-bus!
We fly into the woods.

BIG BROWN BAT
3-6 INCHES LONG

MILLIONS OF BATS!
by Ralphie

Some bats live alone.
Others live in groups.
Millions of bats
can live together!

Even in big groups,
moms can always find their
babies. A mom knows
her baby's cry and smell.

DARK NIGHT
IT'S DINNERTIME!
WHAT DO BATS EAT?
by Carlos
Some bats eat fruit.
Some eat nectar from
flowers. But most bats eat
bugs. One bat can eat more
than 1000 insects in an
hour!
A group of bats can eat
thousands of insects. So,
more bats mean fewer bugs!

EASTERN
RED BAT

HOW BATS CATCH BUGS   by D.A.

Bats use sounds to find things in the dark. They make noises. The noises bounce back to them as echoes.

Bats use the echoes to make a picture in their minds. The picture is just like seeing in the dark.

ECHOLOCATION
Bats locate (find) their food by using echoes.

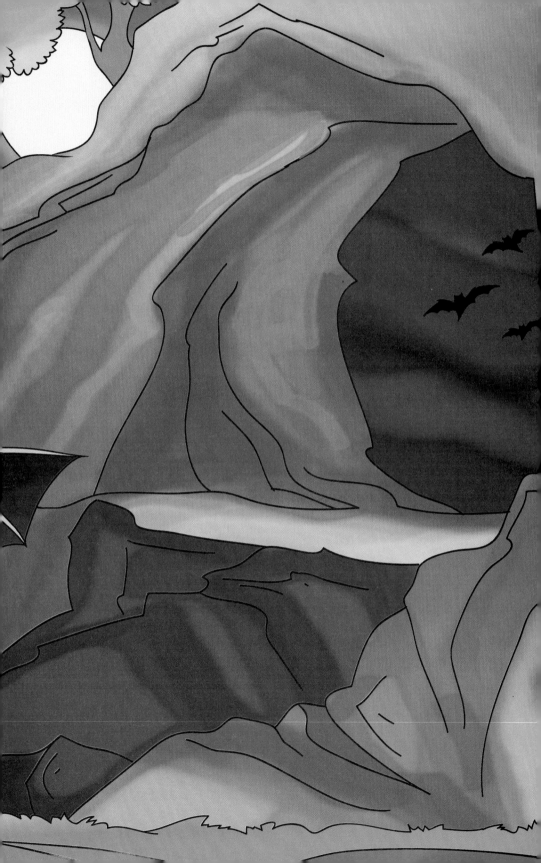

It is dark in the cave.
We can't see any bats.
Then Ms. Frizzle gives us special goggles.
Now we can see them!

Now the bus is just a bus again.
Ms. Frizzle follows the sound to Tim's house.
We see Tim's dad banging a hammer!
He's making a wooden house for the bats.

BATS IN A BAT HOUSE

The little brown bats have a new home.
Now it's time for US to go home.

BATS ARE HELPFUL . . .

Ms. Frizzle is right, bats ARE amazing animals.
- They eat insect pests, like mosquitoes.
- They help pollinate flowers, just like bees.
- Their droppings—also called guano—can be used as fertilizer by farmers.

. . . BUT BE CAREFUL

People still need to be careful around bats—they are wild animals! Never try to touch or handle a wild bat.

LOTS OF BATS

We only mention a few kinds of bats in this book, but there are many kinds of bats. They come in all shapes and sizes and live all over the world.
Here are a few other kinds of bats:

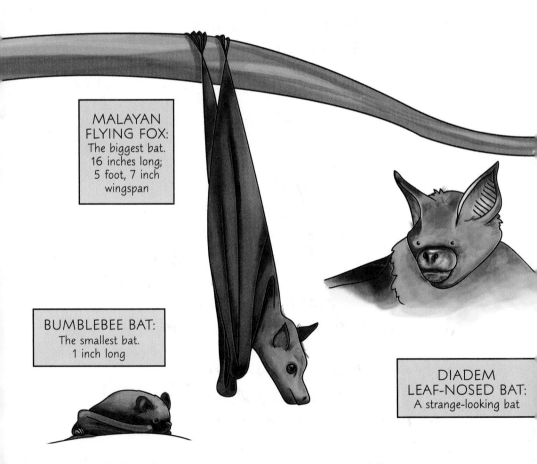

MALAYAN
FLYING FOX:
The biggest bat.
16 inches long;
5 foot, 7 inch
wingspan

BUMBLEBEE BAT:
The smallest bat.
1 inch long

DIADEM
LEAF-NOSED BAT:
A strange-looking bat